PRENTICE HALL DISCOVERIES

FINDING
OUR PLACE IN THE
WORLD

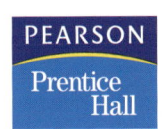

PEARSON
Prentice Hall

Boston, Massachusetts
Upper Saddle River, New Jersey

Copyright © 2007 by Pearson Education, Inc., publishing as Prentice Hall, Boston, Massachusetts 02116. All rights reserved. Printed in the United States of America. This publication is protected by copyright, and permission should be obtained from the publisher prior to any prohibited reproduction, storage in a retrieval system, or transmission in any form or by any means, electronic, mechanical, photocopying, recording, or likewise. For information regarding permission(s), write to: Rights and Permissions Department, One Lake Street, Upper Saddle River, New Jersey 07458.

Pearson Prentice Hall™ is a trademark of Pearson Education, Inc.

Pearson® is a registered trademark of Pearson plc.

Prentice Hall® is a registered trademark of Pearson Education, Inc.

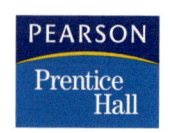

ISBN 0-13-363637-2

3 V059 10

PRENTICE HALL DISCOVERIES

Finding Our Place in the World

What should we learn?

Table of Contents

Social Studies Connection:
Stonehenge: Groundbreaking Discoveries   4

◎ *Learning about ancient civilizations gives us clues to who we are.*

Science Connection:
Where on Earth Are You?   22

◎ *Learning about GPS and other tracking methods will help us figure out where we are and where we are going.*

Humanities Connection:
From Bricks and Mortar to Cyberspace:
Art Museums Online   40

◎ *Learning about fine art gives us insight into the cultures and people who produced it.*

Mathematics Connection:
Testing the Market   58

◎ *Learning about the market for products helps us decide what to produce.*

Glossary   76

STONEHENGE
GROUNDBREAKING DISCOVERIES

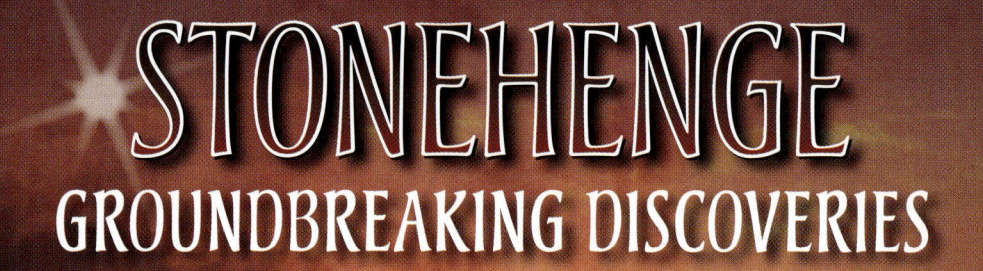

The science of archaeology **focuses** on ancient people and cultures. Archaeologists **explore** the ruins of ancient buildings and graves. They dig for artifacts, such as tools and pottery, from the past. These **crucial** clues help scientists discover ways in which people once lived.

We can learn a great deal from the work of archaeologists. Knowing about the past **enriches** our own lives. It **enables** us to better understand our customs, values, and ways of life.

Sunrise Over Stonehenge

It is the summer solstice, the Northern Hemisphere's longest day of the year. Here, along the emerald, blustery plains of southern England, an archaeologist contemplates the past. She sits silently in the stillness before a circle of monoliths. The visitor wonders about the people who built it so long ago.

The visitor observes the **radiant** sunrise. She **reacts** in wonder as the sun's rays pour **profusely** through a stone archway. Now, as she watches, the sun moves toward its place in the heavens.

Below the bright orb, the ancient circle of standing stones, called Stonehenge, aligns precisely with the sunrise. This alignment is no accident. In fact, the visitor knows that it is very **significant**. The monoliths, she is certain, were purposely arranged to highlight the sunrise.

VOCABULARY

focus (FOH kuhs) *v.* to fix or concentrate on one thing; adjust to make clear

explore (eks PLOHR) *v.* look into closely; examine carefully

crucial (KROO shuhl) *adj.* important; critical

enrich (en RICH) *v.* give more value or effectiveness to

enable (en AY buhl) *v.* make able; authorize, allow, or permit

radiant (RAY dee uhnt) *adj.* shining brightly

react (ree AKT) *v.* behave in a particular way in response to someone or something

profusely (proh FYOOS lee) *adv.* freely; plentifully; excessively

significant (sig NIF i kuhnt) *adj.* having an important meaning

A map of Great Britain showing the location of Stonehenge

Ancient Builders

The visitor is an archaeologist. She considers the purpose of the ancient site. For years, experts **presumed** Stonehenge to be an early observatory or an astronomical calendar. Some people believe it stands as a tribute to the seasons.

Stonehenge is one of the world's most mystifying prehistoric sites. It towers over Salisbury Plain in southern England. Today, it lies in ruins. Yet, it remains a treasure.

The construction of Stonehenge first began 5,000 years ago, during the Stone Age. Stonehenge must have been extremely important to past residents of Salisbury Plain. Its building, which took place in stages, continued for about 1,500 years.

The construction shows the incredible ingenuity and **aptitude** of its **anonymous** engineers. Lacking the tools and technology that we **rely** on today, the ancient builders used available natural resources to build their own tools. They crafted axes from deer antlers. They used the shoulder blades of cattle as a kind of rake. They relied on simple ropes, rollers, levers—and sheer human strength—to move building materials.

Vocabulary

presume (pree ZOOM) *v.* accept something as true until proven otherwise

aptitude (AP tuh tood) *n.* ability or talent

anonymous (uh NAHN uh muhs) *adj.* by someone whose name is withheld or unknown; unacknowledged

rely (ree LY) *v.* trust or depend on someone or something

Weighty Problems

The very building of Stonehenge is indeed a wonder. Consider the 80 or so gigantic bluestones used in construction more than 4,000 years ago. Workers first quarried the stones from the Preseli Mountains of Wales.

These bluish-gray stones certainly must have presented hefty problems for the builders. Some stones could weigh over 4 tons (4 metric tons). They had to be moved 155 miles (250 km), not an **insignificant** distance, from Wales to Stonehenge.

How did workers do it? They probably lugged the stones on rollers and sledges. Did builders next float the stones on river rafts or boats to **transport** them to Stonehenge? Scientists believe that this method is a likely possibility.

Some years later workers added large sedimentary rocks to Stonehenge. These are called sarsens. The giant rocks came from Marlborough Downs, about 20 miles (30 km) away. Yet, neither weight nor distance **hindered** the ambitious workers.

These sarsen stones are like those used in Stonehenge.

Experts think that the workers hauled the rocks over land using ropes made of cow's hair. They lugged them onto timber tracks. Then, the builders **cooperated** to hoist the stones onto platforms built of wooden planks. Finally, they labored together to arrange the stones, the bulkiest of which weighed a staggering 55 tons (50 metric tons).

Whichever methods of transportation and positioning these ancient people employed, it is awe-inspiring to realize how adept and resourceful they were. Just as we do today, they had to plan, cooperate, and labor to accomplish their remarkable feat.

However, recently Stonehenge may have become a bit less mystifying. A new **discovery** nearby has been archaeologists' **impetus** in rethinking the purpose of the monoliths. Like winds whipping across the **desolate** Salisbury Plain, exciting new theories are gaining momentum.

Vocabulary

insignificant (IN sig NIF i kuhnt) *adj.* having little or no meaning

transport (tranz POHRT) *v.* to carry or move from one place to another

hindered (HIN derd) *v.* held back

cooperate (koh AHP er AYT) *v.* work together with others for a common purpose

discovery (di SKUV uh ree) *n.* a fact, thing, or answer to a question that someone discovers, or finds

impetus (IM puh tuhs) *n.* driving force

desolate (DES uh lit) *adj.* lonely; solitary

A Village Unearthed

In 2006, scientists **unearthed** another wonder called Durrington Walls. This site lies in a valley 1.75 miles (2.8 km) northeast of Stonehenge. In it, archaeologists have uncovered a prehistoric village. Some have called it a suburb of Stonehenge.

Like Stonehenge, the village is a henge, or circular area. Encircled with a ditch and a bank, it is 1,400 feet (427 m) wide. Carbon dating reveals that the village was built around 2600–2500 B.C. That is about the same time that the sarsen stones were brought to Stonehenge.

Today, Durrington is the site of ongoing investigation. Scientists continue to dig for clues to **investigate** its past.

In 2005, scientists had uncovered a stone roadway. Called an "avenue" by archaeologists, the 90-foot-wide (27 m), 560-foot-long (170 m) road leads from the settlement to the River Avon. A twin avenue at neighboring Stonehenge also links to the river.

During that year and the next, scientists exposed a total of eight prehistoric huts in the village. The huts were made of wood. Square or nearly rectangular in shape, each contained a hearth, or fireplace. In the well-preserved clay floors, scientists **identified** outlines where wooden beds, cupboards, and other furniture once stood.

Through surveys of the surprisingly small site, experts believe that several hundred houses probably jammed the valley in close clusters. At one time, the valley swarmed with people.

Vocabulary

unearthed (un ERTHD) *v.* dug up

investigate (in VES tuh GAYT) *v.* examine an object or situation in order to gain information

identify (eye DEN tuh FY) *v.* recognize something and be able to say what it is

This photo shows the clay floors of the village that were uncovered by scientists.

In the dig, scientists also discovered two unusual houses. These dwellings had been built apart from the others. They were set on a terrace, which offered spectacular views of the River Avon. Why were these buildings given such a prime location? Professor Mike Parker Pearson, a British archaeologist, heads the excavation. He studies ancient burial practices. He believes that these homes may have housed chiefs or priests.

Another archaeologist, Julian Thomas, says they may have been shrines, or places of worship or ritual. Thomas suggests that people may have visited these two homes to **connect** with their ancestral spirits.

Unlike the other dwellings unearthed, the floors of these two have worn away over the ages, leaving behind only their hearths—and more questions.

Treasures in the Trash

It is often said that one person's garbage is another's treasure. For archaeologists, trash is treasure. At the dig, scientists sift through mounds of ancient garbage. The rubbish offers valuable clues to the past.

Professor Parker Pearson commented on the trash at Durrington. He said, "This is the richest—and by that I mean the filthiest—site of this period known in Britain. We've never seen such quantities of pottery and animal bones and flint."

Arrowheads uncovered near Stonehenge

The dig also uncovered jewelry and arrowheads. It revealed charred cooking stones along with the flints. People used the flint to create sparks for building fires. In a kitchen midden, or garbage heap, scientists also found bones from domestic pigs and cattle. Some bones still contained the arrowheads used to kill the animals.

Vocabulary

connect (kuh NEKT) *v.* to join or be joined

Large, unbutchered sections of bones uncovered in the dig indicated that people ate—excessively. In fact, Professor Parker Pearson noted, "The animal bones were being thrown away half eaten." This indicates that food was so plentiful that people wasted it. They cast bones to the floor. Now, ages later, archaeological treasure hunters retrieve them as if they were bars of gold.

In the garbage, scientists found human bones, too. They also discovered evidence of animal sacrifice.

Surprisingly, what scientists did not find is also relevant to learning about life thousands of years ago. For

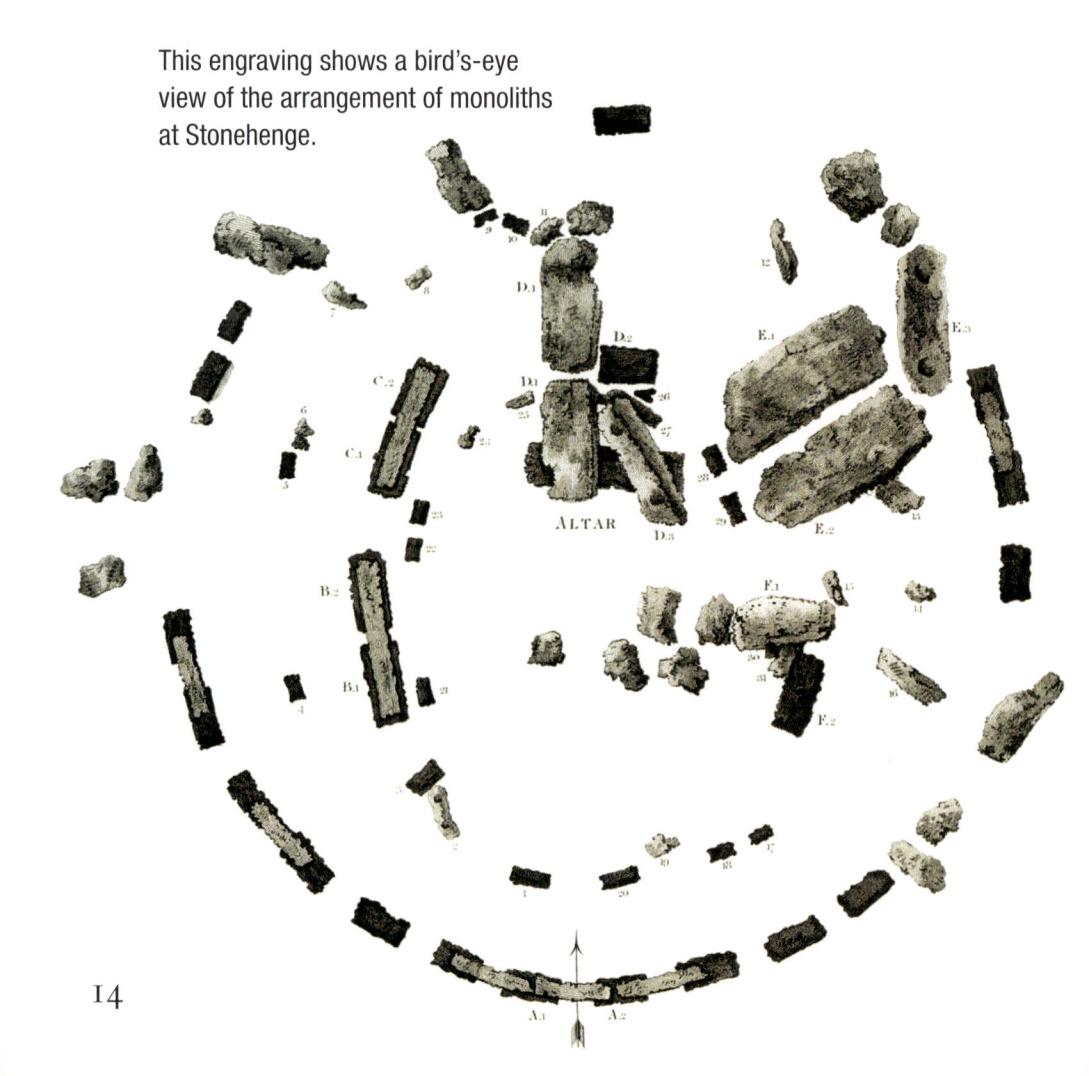

This engraving shows a bird's-eye view of the arrangement of monoliths at Stonehenge.

example, the archaeologists did not find utensils for scraping animal hides. They did not find evidence of querns. These were used to grind grains by hand. They did not find carbonized grain.

How is the absence of these household items **relevant**? It led scientists to conclude that this village was not a place where people performed typical daily activities. Instead, the village was a temporary resting place. It was a home away from home. It was intended for furious feasting and funeral rituals. Professor Parker Pearson explained, "It's completely different from any other Neolithic settlement assemblage we've ever looked at before."

Connecting Durrington and Stonehenge

What else do the excavations tell us about the lives—and deaths—of the ancients? Plenty, if you ask the archaeologists. Professor Parker Pearson believes that, together, Stonehenge and Durrington Walls formed a type of sacred compound. He stated, "Durrington is almost a mirror image of its stone counterpart at Stonehenge." Further, he **emphasized**, "Stonehenge isn't a monument in isolation. It is actually one of a pair—one in stone, one in timber."

Vocabulary

relevant (REL uh vuhnt) *adj.* having a logical connection with; relating to the point

emphasize (EM fuh syz) *v.* stress something in order to make it stand out

15

A most intriguing feature that Durrington Walls and Stonehenge share is that both align with key points in the astronomical calendar. Durrington Walls aligns with the winter solstice sunrise. Stonehenge aligns with the sunset. On the summer solstice, Stonehenge aligns with the sunrise and Durrington aligns with the sunset.

Their alignment on the solstice may indicate that large parties took place at these times. Professor Parker Pearson theorizes that people throughout the region gathered together for the winter solstice in a **communal** celebration of life.

Vocabulary

communal (kuh MYOON uhl) *adj.* shared by all

Stonehenge aligns with the winter solstice sunrise and the summer solstice sunset.

This image combines four photos that show Stonehenge at night and four phases of the moon.

During the festivities, people traveled from Durrington Walls to Stonehenge. They first feasted at Durrington. The great number of bones suggests evidence of such seasonal feasts. That conclusion makes perfect sense. Think about the large amount of chicken or rib bones people today might discard after a holiday dinner, a large family gathering, or a birthday celebration.

After feasting, they laid their dead to rest at Stonehenge. Professor Parker Pearson believes that people journeyed along the stone roadway, or avenue, to the River Avon.

Then, they transported their dead over the river, which carried the dead away to the afterlife—symbolized by Stonehenge. There, the people cremated and buried the dead. Stonehenge, Parker Pearson thinks, was a memorial to the departed, as revealed by the large amount of human remains buried there.

Scientists have noted the symbolic nature of the building materials of the two sites. Made of timber, Durrington illustrates the frail nature of life. In contrast, rocky Stonehenge symbolizes permanent death—something all people must face.

For archaeologists, these latest findings have indeed

made a huge difference in the way they view Stonehenge. Mike Pitts, editor of the magazine *British Archaeology,* sums it up. "For the very first time, it's creating a social world into which we can place Stonehenge," he explained.

As we **evaluate** what it means to be social human beings, these monuments offer us valuable insight into the people of the past. They embraced life with feasts.

> **VOCABULARY**
>
> **evaluate** (ee VAL yoo AYT) *v.* examine something to make a judgment

This family enjoys a Thanksgiving feast, just as the ancient people feasted at Durrington Walls.

They honored their dead in burial rituals. Their celebration of life reminds us to celebrate our own. Their respect for those who died reminds us to remain connected to the past. The sites also remind us to find connections to the human beings who, long, long ago, created significant monuments.

Thanks to groundbreaking discoveries, we are able to learn how an ancient culture celebrated life and honored death. Excavations at Durrington are expected to continue through 2010. New discoveries and new theories will help us gain greater insight into the people who once lived on Salisbury Plain and reveled in the radiant sunrise of a solstice morning. Like the sun, continued excavations will shed new light on ancient cultures.

Discussion Questions

1. Stonehenge was once considered an ancient observatory, an astronomical calendar, or a tribute to the seasons. How have recent excavations caused scientists to rethink its purpose?

2. What did the items contained in Durrington's trash heaps reveal? How did what scientists did *not* find reveal information, too?

3. How can learning about a past civilization help us better understand our own?

WHERE ON EARTH ARE YOU?

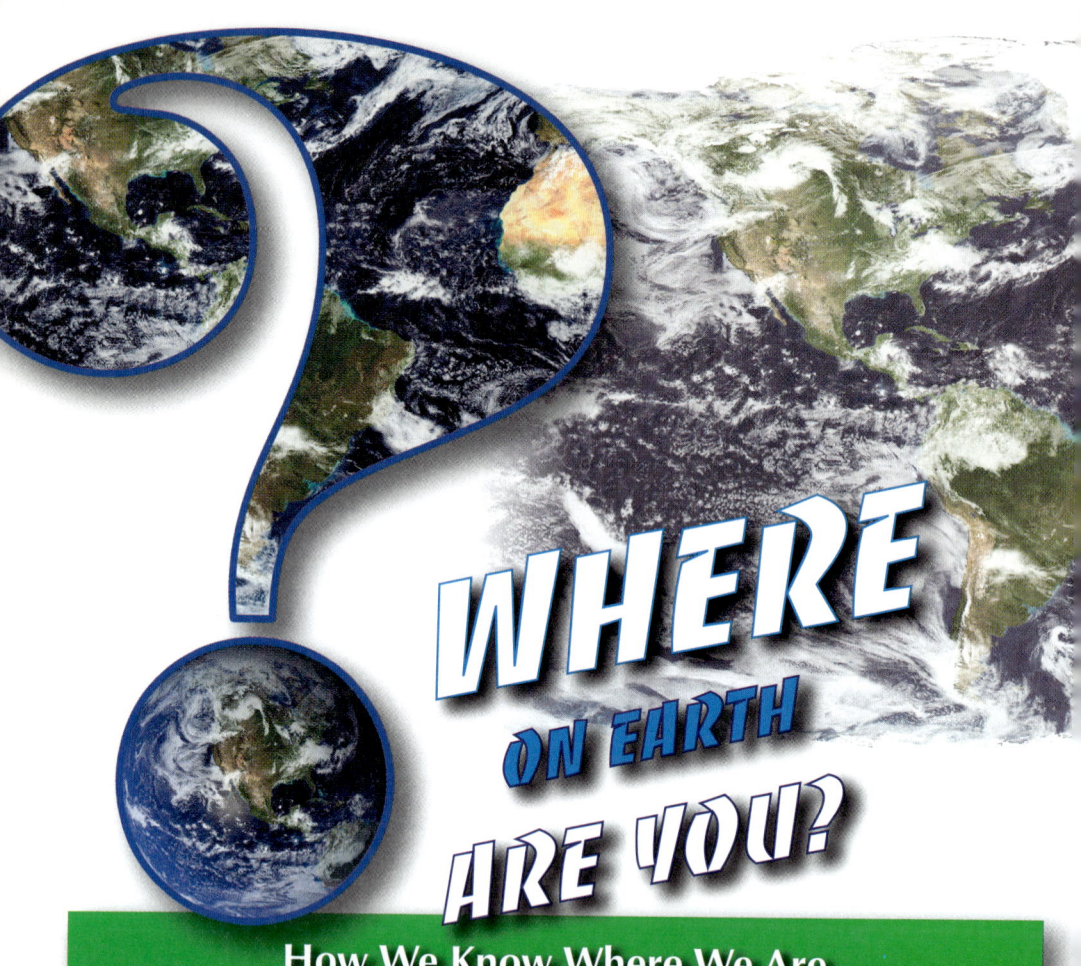

How We Know Where We Are

It's a big planet. Finding your way around it can be trickier than you think. However, over the years people have developed amazing ways to **identify** their position on Earth. Finding your location can be as basic as looking up at the sun and the stars, as sailors discovered hundreds of years ago. It can also be as high-tech as today's most advanced computer systems. But, whichever system people use, each of them helps us to understand and navigate our world a little better.

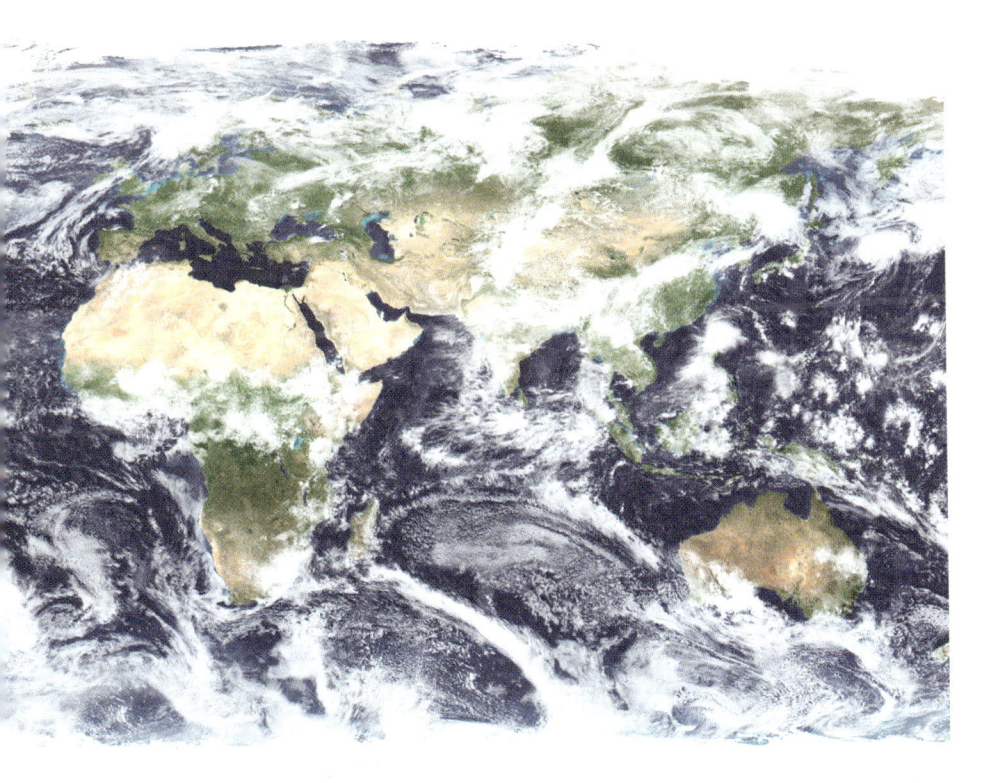

Views of Earth from space

Early Tracking Methods

In the ancient world, few people traveled far from home. When they did, they followed well-known trails and routes. Landmarks and other familiar sights guided their way.

Water was the superhighway of the ancient world. So it is no surprise that the world's first great navigators were seafaring people. At first, most sailors hugged the coastlines. They looked for landmarks such as rocks, reefs, and piers to guide their way.

Vocabulary

identify (eye DEN tuh FY) *v.* recognize something and be able to say what it is

23

Ancient sailors used the sun's position in the sky to aid their navigation.

Over time, boats struck out into open waters. By about A.D. 400, for example, Polynesian sailors had made the **ultimate** long-distance voyage. They traveled more than 2,300 miles (3,700 km) on the open ocean from their South Sea homes to Hawaii.

Without landmarks, the vast sea can be a confusing place—an endless **frontier**. How did the early ocean voyagers find their way?

These explorers looked to the sun. Since the sun rises in the east and sets in the west, travelers could use it to **gauge** direction. For example, if travelers saw the sun on their left in the morning, they knew they were heading south.

Travelers also used direction and distance to draw maps. To **understand** how they might have created a map, imagine living on an island. It takes two days to travel to the nearest island to the north. The islands to the west and east are three- and four-day journeys. Using this data, they might have created a map like the one shown here.

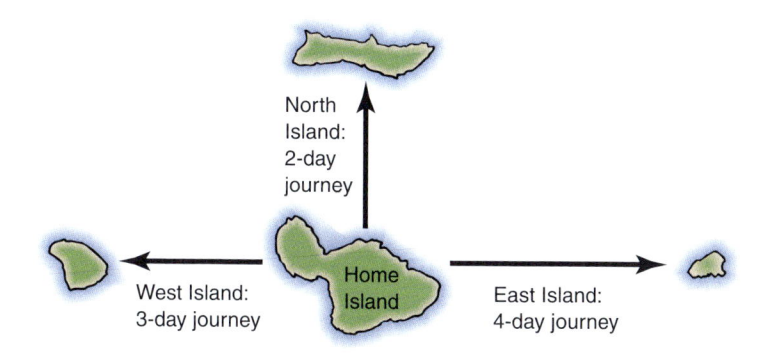

The distance on the map to the east island is about twice the distance to the north island. This plotting makes sense because the time to journey to the east island is twice as long as the time to the north island.

VOCABULARY

ultimate (UHL tuh mit) *adj.* final; last or highest possible

frontier (fruhn TEER) *n.* the developing, often uncivilized, region of a country; any new field of learning

gauge (GAYJ) *v.* estimate; judge

understand (un duhr STAND) *v.* get or perceive the meaning of; know or grasp what is meant; comprehend

Seeing Stars

As sailors **launched** longer voyages, night travel posed a **distinct** problem. Without the sun, how could travelers determine direction? Again, they looked to the sky—this time to the stars. Like the sun, stars seemed to move across the sky over the course of the night. However, unlike the sun, the path of a single star was hard to follow. How could sailors tell any one star from the others?

Luckily, a special star that does not appear to move shines brightly in the north sky. This star, Polaris, became known as the North Star. It **enabled** travelers to find their way at night because it always pointed north.

To understand why Polaris doesn't appear to move, **envision** an imaginary line along Earth's axis. Polaris happens to be located right on that imaginary line. As Earth rotates on its axis, all other stars appear to move in a circle around it. Because Polaris lies directly on the axis, it doesn't appear to move at all.

Sun and Stars: Helpful Partners

By 600 B.C., Mediterranean sailors used both the sun and the stars to **navigate**. To find out how far north or south they were from the equator, they would hold out their arms at noon. Then they measured the sun's height over the horizon in finger-widths. The number of finger-widths told them their location.

To understand how this method worked, imagine standing on the equator. On the diagram, notice where the sun would be shining—directly overhead. It would

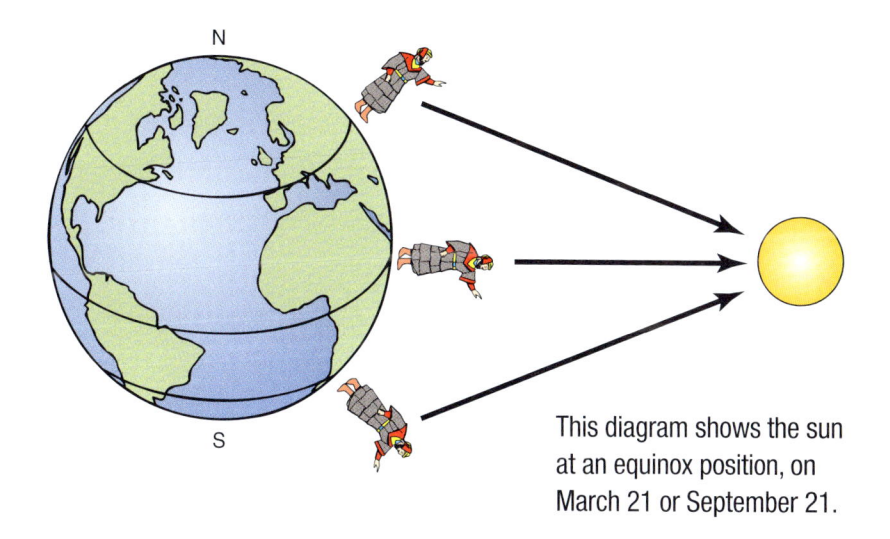

This diagram shows the sun at an equinox position, on March 21 or September 21.

be so high in the sky—and so far from the horizon—you'd need to tilt your head up to see it.

Now imagine standing farther north or south from the equator as the diagram shows. There, the sun shines at a lower angle. You don't need to tilt your head up to see it. In other words, the sun is closer to the horizon and not as high in the sky.

This pattern would continue. The farther north or south you go, the closer the noonday sun would appear to be to the horizon. So you could use this fact to find your position. If the noonday sun appeared high in the sky, you were close to the equator. If the noonday sun was low, you were far from the equator.

Vocabulary

launch (LAWNCH) *v.* start something new; send off a ship, shuttle, or weapon

distinct (dis TINKT) *adj.* separate and different

enable (en AY buhl) *v.* make able; authorize, allow, or permit

envision (en VIZH uhn) *v.* picture in one's mind

navigate (NAV uh gayt) *v.* steer, or direct, a ship or aircraft

27

Rounding Out Earth

All methods of finding north-south locations from the equator **assumed** one **crucial** fact: The Earth was not flat. In fact, most ancient navigators were aware that Earth had a round, ball-like shape. In the 3rd century B.C., one clever Greek mathematician named Eratosthenes [er uh TAS thuh neez] even found a way to measure the distance around the globe.

Eratosthenes measured the angle of the noonday sun at two sites, one 500 miles (805 km) north of the other. He found the sun's angle to be 7 degrees greater at the northernmost location. Seven degrees is about 1/51 of a full 360-degree circle. So Eratosthenes reasoned a full circle to be about 51 times the 500-mile (805 km) distance between the two sites.

Multiplying 51 by 500, Eratosthenes **obtained** a distance around the world of about 25,500 miles (41,038 km). How close was his estimate? Modern science measures Earth's circumference to be about 24,900 miles (40,073 km)!

New Tools

By the 15th century, European sailors had a fairly good image of their world. Ships traveled all over the Mediterranean Sea and north Atlantic Ocean. Pilots **relied** on a variety of instruments to measure and chart their world.

The compass was the first **significant** instrument advance. A compass has a thin magnetic needle that can spin freely on a rod. No matter where you are, a compass always points north.

How does a compass work? Earth itself has a large magnetic field running along its north-south axis. The compass needle simply lines up with this north-south field.

Other instruments that were **indispensable** to navigators included the astrolabe and sextant. These tools could accurately measure north-south position using the sun. But they were not reliable for measuring east or west positions. It wasn't until the 18th century that navigators found a dependable way to do such measurements.

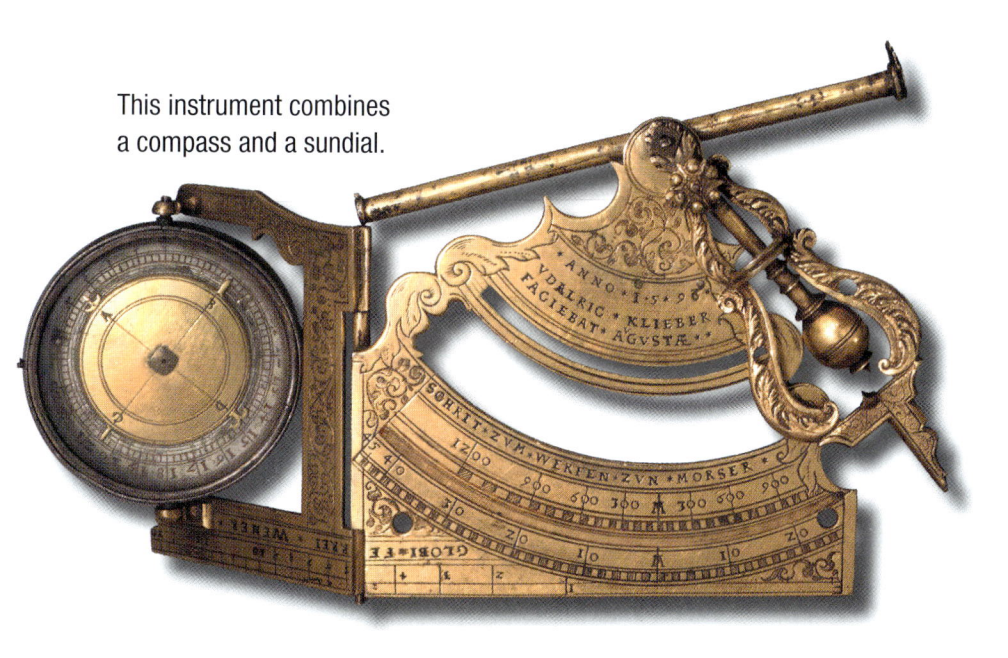

This instrument combines a compass and a sundial.

Vocabulary

assume (uh SOOM) *v.* suppose something to be a fact; take on, as in a responsibility or role

crucial (KROO shuhl) *adj.* important; critical

obtain (uhb TAYN) *v.* gain possession of something

rely (ree LY) *v.* trust or depend on someone or something

significant (sig NIF i kuhnt) *adj.* having an important meaning

indispensable (IN di SPEN suh buhl) *adj.* absolutely necessary, can't be thrown away

Mad About Maps

In the Middle Ages, people did not **emphasize** education. As a result, knowledge of the Earth's round shape got lost. Once again, many people came to believe that the Earth was flat. This mistaken idea began to change when 15th-century printers rediscovered the maps of a Greek Egyptian named Ptolemy [TAHL uh mee].

Ptolemy's maps were originally drawn in the 2nd century A.D. They had been lost for more than a thousand years! Even so, Ptolemy included key features that other 15th-century maps lacked. He added longitudes and latitudes, for example, although he was not quite accurate.

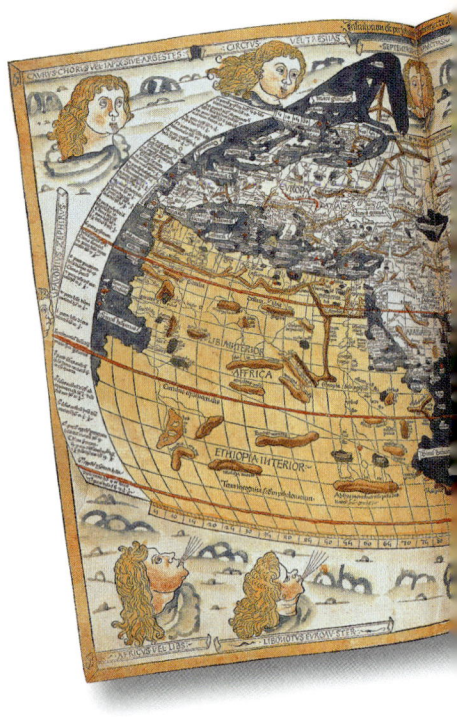

This 1486 map of the world was based on a much earlier map by Ptolemy.

Longitudes and latitudes are imaginary lines that circle the globe. Longitudes run north and south. Latitudes are **parallel** and run east and west. Using these lines, each position on Earth can be located and **checked** like a street address. The location system starts at zero for north-south positions on the equator. The zero-line for longitude is located in England. For example, Atlanta, Georgia, is located at latitude N33, longitude 84W. So, Atlanta is 33 degrees north of the equator (zero latitude) and 84 degrees west of England's zero-longitude.

Trouble with Longitude

In 1492, Columbus's famous voyage **demonstrated** that Earth was a sphere. In the following years, new world maps began to appear. These maps were much more accurate than Ptolemy's maps. However, as late as the 18th century, navigators and mapmakers still had a great deal of trouble finding east-west positions, or longitudes.

In theory, measuring longitude wasn't hard. In one 24-hour day Earth spins at a rate that covers a full 360-degree rotation. So, each hour the Earth's position changes by 15 degrees. Using this fact, you can measure longitude—if you have an accurate clock.

Suppose, for example, you set your clock for London time and sail west. After a few days, you don't know how far west you've sailed. However, you do know that when you see the sun at its noonday position, your London clock reads 1:00 P.M.

VOCABULARY

emphasize (EM fuh syz) *v.* stress something in order to make it stand out

parallel (PAR uh lel) *adj.* extending in the same direction and at the same distance apart

check (CHEK) *v.* confirm that something is true or accurate

demonstrate (DEM uhn strayt) *v.* show or make clear by using examples or modeling

Since the sun tells you that it's high noon where you are, you know your time is exactly one hour behind London time. Since one hour translates to 15 degrees, you are 15 degrees west of London. In distance, 15 degrees equals about 2,000 miles (3,219 km).

There was one problem with the "clock method" for finding longitude at sea. Eighteenth-century clocks were not accurate! In 1707, a British sea captain calculated longitude incorrectly using this method. He thought he had safely avoided treacherous rocks near some islands. Instead, his ships ran directly into them. His fleet sank only a few miles from home.

"Never again!" the British government declared. It then **contributed** 20,000 pounds to be offered as a prize for a contest. Anyone who could invent a quick and reliable method for measuring longitude at sea would win the splendid prize. The reward would be worth millions of dollars today.

In 1720, John Harrison **undertook** the challenge to build an accurate portable clock. No one would have **predicted** success for this unknown British clockmaker. For 52 years, Harrison worked on his clock, which he named H4. Rivals tried to cheat him. Contest officials refused to give him the prize even after it was clear he deserved it. Fortunately, Harrison was an **optimist**. He didn't give up. In 1773, the government finally awarded Harrison the prize. The King of England himself presented the prize money!

Harrison's clock was the final piece of the puzzle. From the 18th century on, navigation improved enormously. Guesswork was no longer **required**.

John Harrison solved the problem of how to determine longitude at sea.

Vocabulary

contribute (kuhn TRIB yoot) *v.* give or share money, knowledge, or ideas

undertake (UN her TAYK) *v.* take on or agree to do a difficult or lengthy task

predict (pree DIKT) *v.* say in advance what you think will happen; foretell

optimist (AHP tuh mist) *n.* someone who takes the most hopeful view of matters

require (ree KWYR) *v.* demand by law; deem necessary

Finding Location in the Twentieth Century

Even before the age of computers, 20th-century sailors had reliable ways to find their locations. One was triangulation. The diagrams show how this method works.

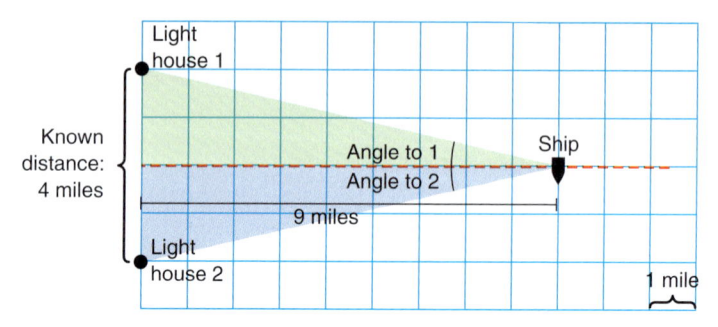

TRIANGULATION
1. Ship position is SOMEWHERE on the dotted red line
2. Ship sights 2 lighthouses 4 miles apart
3. Navigator measures angles
4. Scale drawing shows distance to shore: 9 miles

Using triangulation, the ship's pilot can determine that the ship is 9 miles from land.

Imagine a ship located somewhere offshore between two known landmarks, for example, two lighthouses. The ship's pilot doesn't know how far the ship is from the shore. However, she does know that the lighthouses are 4 miles apart.

The pilot measures the angle to each lighthouse. Then she draws the angles on paper. Each box on the paper represents 1 mile. The pilot extends the angles until they meet. This spot, where they meet, marks the ship's location. To find the distance from shore, the pilot now counts the number of boxes. The ship is 9 miles from land.

Another way to find a ship's position is using moon and sun readings. A pilot in the Atlantic would first take a reading of the moon's position. A chart that maps the moon's position for every moment of every day gives the pilot directions for drawing the large blue circle shown on the map. The ship is located somewhere on this blue circle.

To get the exact position, the pilot now measures the angle of the sun and draws the red circle. The ship's location is at one of the two points where the circles intersect. Because only one of the two points is located in the same hemisphere as the ship, that point marks the location of the ship.

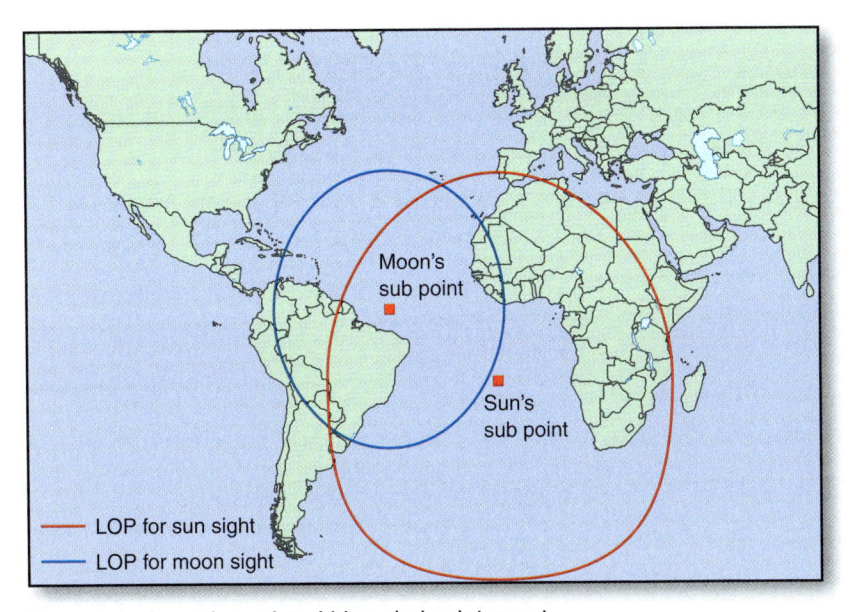

The point where the red and blue circles intersect is the location of the ship.

This satellite photo shows part of the city of New Orleans after Hurricane Katrina.

Computer Mapping Programs

For the most part, 21st-century navigators don't need charts and tables anymore. At a click of a mouse, computer mapping programs can zoom in on almost every location on the planet. All that is needed is a computer and an Internet connection.

Suppose you want to view your neighborhood. The mapping program starts with a view of Earth from outer space. You type in your address. The program "skydives" right in to your state, town, and block where you live. It even locates your house!

Is this view of your location live? No. The program uses satellite photographs to create a map. Thousands of satellites and aircraft take millions of pictures of Earth. The computer puts all of these images together to make a complete picture.

Global Positioning System

The ultimate computer map is a Global Positioning System (GPS). GPS combines an incredibly accurate positioning system with an incredibly accurate mapping system. Some GPS systems are on target to within 6 feet (2 m).

In operation, a GPS system instantly locates you—or your car—on a map. A symbol on the map represents you. As you move in the real world, that symbol moves with you.

How does GPS **achieve** this amazing feat? Orbiting satellites send signals that the GPS receiver picks up. Each signal allows the computer to draw a mapping

Vocabulary

achieve (uh CHEEV) *v.* succeed in doing something; accomplish; gain

sphere on a three-dimensional map of the space surrounding Earth. You must receive signals from three different satellites to find your position. The place on the map where the three mapping spheres intersect marks your location.

At the speed of light, the signal from satellite 1 travels to the receiver in 0.06 seconds. Multiplying the speed of light by 0.06 seconds indicates that your receiver on Earth is 11,160 miles (17,960 km) from the satellite. So your location could be anywhere on the mapping sphere surrounding satellite 1.

Your receiver now picks up signals from satellites 2 and 3. The computer draws a separate mapping sphere for each satellite.

Now the computer **analyzes** the data. The three spheres intersect at more than one point. The computer rules out intersection points that lie in outer space. Only one position lies on Earth. So that's where you are!

This handheld GPS device can help drivers travel in unfamiliar areas without getting lost.

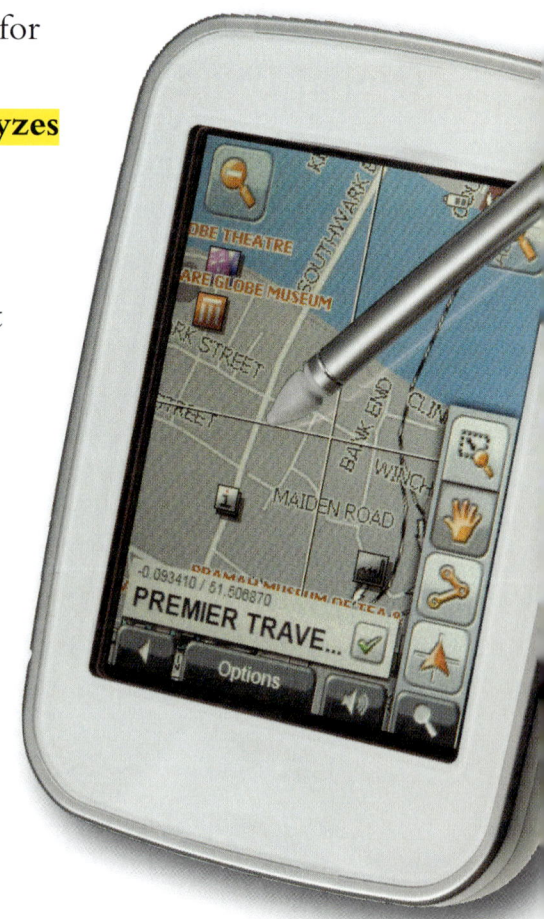

Is GPS the be-all and end-all of finding location? Perhaps. However, skilled navigators know how to read the heavens and charts and maps. They know how to use instruments and computers. All of these methods allow us to understand the physical world we live in. They also help us to **define** who we are.

Discussion Questions

1. How did early travelers use the sun and the stars to navigate?

2. Suppose you were on a boat in the open ocean with no land in sight. Without a computer or GPS, how could you determine your position?

3. Describe why it was easier for navigators to make north-south position measurements than east–west measurements. How did Harrison's clock change the situation?

4. Describe two 21st-century systems for finding location. Do you think you can rely on these systems?

Vocabulary

analyze (AN uh lyz) *v.* break something down into parts to examine it or determine its nature

define (dee FYN) *v.* set clear boundaries or distinct characteristics

From Bricks and Mortar to Cyberspace

Art Museums Online

When I look at an artist's drawing of an animal, I learn something about that creature. I stare at a cat painted on the wall of an ancient Egyptian tomb. It does not look the same as a cat drawn by Andy Warhol, an artist who lived in modern America. Why? Place and time shape the artist's mind and train the artist's hand. Art reflects the world of its creator.

HUMANITIES

The world's art **museums** offer us rich opportunities to learn about our world through art. Wouldn't it be wonderful to be able to travel the world to visit the great art museums? Unfortunately, not all of us can be worldwide travelers. Luckily though, through modern technology, we can all **transport** ourselves anywhere in the world to online art museums both great and small.

The Art Museum

When I **envision** a traditional art museum, I imagine a grand building. It looks like a palace. In fact, some of today's art museums once belonged to kings and queens. The Louvre in Paris, France—home of the "Mona Lisa"—is now one of the most famous museums in the world. However, at one time, its art belonged to the royalty who collected it. Ordinary art lovers had little opportunity to see the art. Today much of the world's great art is housed in museums that are open to the public.

These museums collect and display art that experts believe will have lasting cultural value. Most museums own some of the work they display. This work is called a permanent collection. Some of the collection is always on display. Some of it, however, is on display only occasionally. It sits in storage the rest of the time. A museum

VOCABULARY

museum (myoo ZEE uhm) *n.* institution, building, or room for preserving and exhibiting artistic, historical, or scientific objects

transport (tranz POHRT) *v.* to carry or move from one place to another

envision (en VIZH uhn) *v.* picture in one's mind

might also display art that is loaned to it for a limited time. In other words, the exhibits in a museum change.

Both actual museums and their websites vary their exhibits. In fact, online exhibits and features usually change more often than those in a brick-and-mortar museum. What I saw on my virtual travels this morning could easily be gone by this evening.

From Bricks and Mortar to Bytes and Pixels

Art can **enrich** the lives of all who experience it. Museums want to break down the barriers that have **hindered** people's access to art. Using the Internet is one way museums **promote** their programs to wider audiences. When the Internet was new, a major museum might use a website to give only the most basic **information**. If I were planning an **expedition** to New York City, for instance, I could use the website of the Metropolitan Museum of Art—called the Met, for short—to find its address and hours.

Thanks to **significant** technical advances, nearly every museum can now **launch** a website. That site can do much more than publish a museum's address and hours. Museums can post high quality images of art online. They can also offer virtual tours, videos, audios, and games. On a recent online visit to the Met, I discovered a site that has gone way beyond the basics.

Vocabulary

enrich (en RICH) *v.* give more value or effectiveness to

hindered (HIN derd) *v.* held back

promote (pruh MOHT) *v.* encourage; contribute to the growth of; raise to a higher level or rank

information (in fuhr MAY shuhn) *n.* knowledge; facts; data

expedition (eks puh DI shuhn) *n.* journey taken for a specific purpose

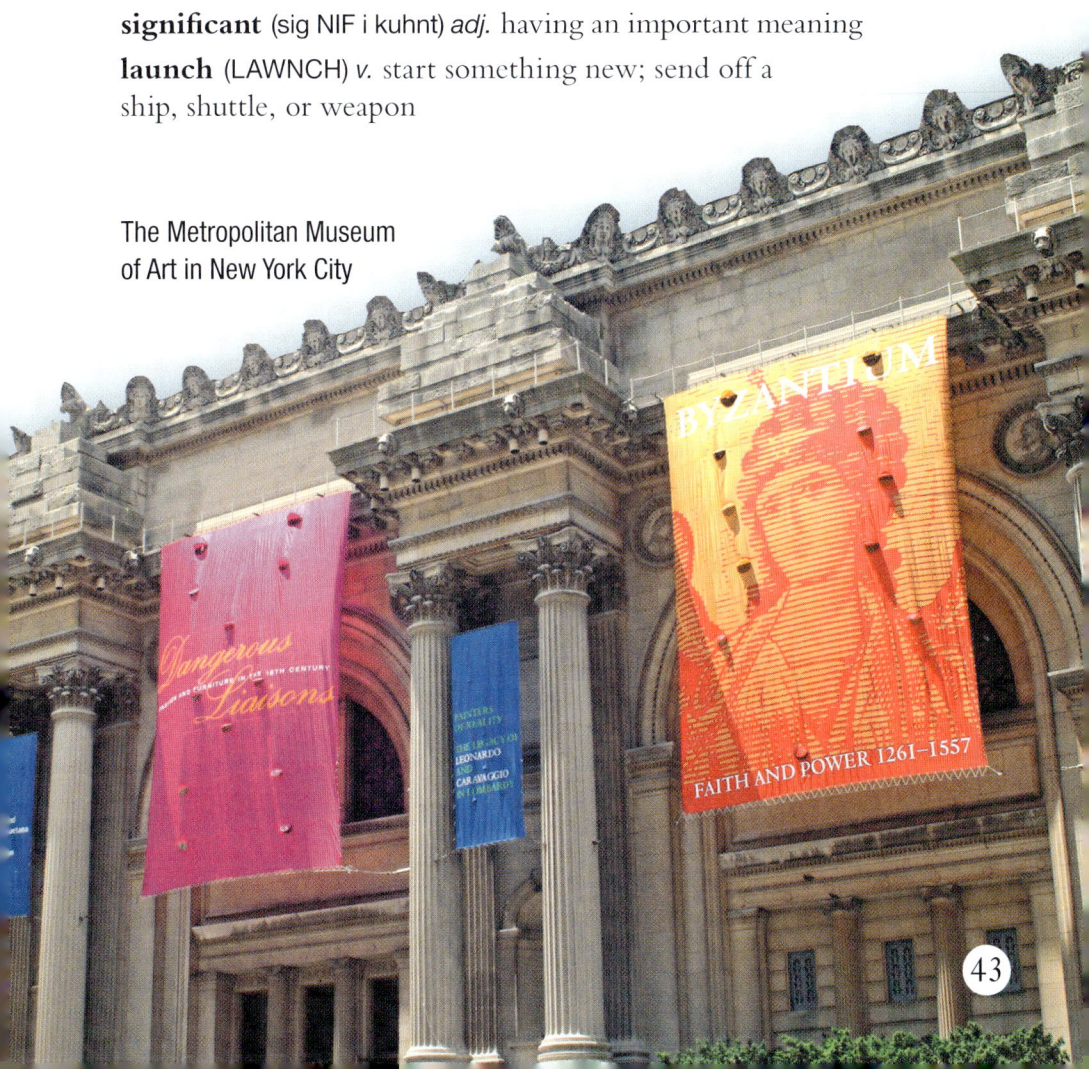

significant (sig NIF i kuhnt) *adj.* having an important meaning

launch (LAWNCH) *v.* start something new; send off a ship, shuttle, or weapon

The Metropolitan Museum of Art in New York City

The Metropolitan Museum of Art Online

The Met has two million works of art in its collection. About 6,500 of them can be viewed online. On my recent virtual visit, I browsed the collection of American paintings. Since I like animals, I decided to **focus** on a work called "Lady with Her Pets" by Rufus Hathaway.

I clicked to enlarge the image of the painting. Then, I used the zoom feature to **analyze** the details of the painting. I looked closely at the bird on the back of the chair. I saw a robin! Then, I **identified** the bird perched in the ring. I saw a parrot. Finally, I looked at the flying creatures in the upper corner. They were either butterflies or moths. I almost missed the lady's black cat staring out from the bottom left. What an unusual collection of pets! What **impressed** me the most, however, was the lady's very peculiar hairstyle.

I read the caption under the painting. It told me the birth and death dates of the artist Rufus Hathaway and the date of the painting—1790. I wanted some **elaboration** on these facts. So, I clicked on the artist's name and found a paragraph on Hathaway and his work. I learned that the hairstyle of the lady in the painting was a French fashion trend of the time. I'm glad that trend didn't last!

After analyzing the "Lady with Her Pets," I decided to find out what special features for kids the Met online might have. From a list of several appealing offerings, I chose to explore a colorful collage by artist Romare Bearden. In seconds, I was on a virtual guided tour through this New York City neighborhood. All the while, I was listening to some cool jazz, too!

This oil painting, *Lady with Her Pets*, can be seen at the Metropolitan Museum of Art Online.

Vocabulary

focus (FOH kuhs) *v.* to fix or concentrate on one thing; adjust to make clear

analyze (AN uh lyz) *v.* break something down into parts to examine it or determine its nature

identify (eye DEN tuh FY) *v.* recognize something and be able to say what it is

impress (im PRES) *v.* make someone feel admiration and respect; make clear the importance

elaboration (ee LAB uh RAY shuhn) *n.* adding of more details

45

The J. Paul Getty Museum Online

In the blink of an eye and the click of a mouse, I moved from New York to Los Angeles to visit the Getty. Clicking on "Explore Art," I browsed by subject. The theme "People and Occupations" caught my eye.

From a menu of options, I clicked "Entertainers." Tiny images of musicians, clowns, and other entertainers filled the screen. I then chose "Statuette of Comic Actor." An **anonymous** Greek artist created this small clay statue more than 2,000 years ago. I wanted to **examine** it from different angles. If I had really been standing in front of this statue, I would have circled it. To my delight, I could do almost the same thing while sitting comfortably at home. All I had to do was click on three different views of the funny little figure with the wide grin.

Like the Met, the Getty offers online activities that are both fun and educational. When I visited the "GettyGames" page, I played "Detail Detective," "Match Madness," and "Switch." Each activity encouraged me to look more closely at art. I could play the games at two levels—"hard" and "not so hard." I recommend warming up on the "not so hard" level. These games aren't as easy as they look! After building a jigsaw puzzle of beautiful flowers painted by Vincent van Gogh, I decided to learn something about art conservation.

We **rely** on museums to **conserve** art for future generations. Museums must protect art from extreme temperatures and other conditions that might damage it. They also **undertake** the cleaning and repair of art. When I read the web page of the Getty's Research and

Marion True is the curator of antiquities at the Getty Museum. Here she is shown with an ancient statue in a museum warehouse.

Conservation department, I learned that this museum also conserves art outside of its own collection. The Getty experts have even worked on the exotic Great Sphinx in Egypt!

Vocabulary

anonymous (uh NAHN uh muhs) *adj.* by someone whose name is withheld or unknown; unacknowledged

examine (eg ZAM uhn) *v.* look at carefully in order to find out the facts and condition of something; inspect

rely (ree LY) *v.* trust or depend on someone or something

conserve (kuhn SERV) *v.* keep from being damaged, lost, or wasted; save

undertake (UN her TAYK) *v.* take on or agree to do a difficult or lengthy task

The State Hermitage Museum

How long would it take to travel thousands of miles from the Getty in Los Angeles, California, to the Hermitage in St. Petersburg, Russia? Traveling nonstop by plane could take about 10 hours. Traveling through cyberspace, I got there in a split second.

Like the Louvre, the Hermitage is a museum that was once a palace. Built in the 18th century to be the home of Russian tsars, the magnificent buildings were closed to the public. Today, anyone can walk freely through the doors of the Hermitage. I walked through the museum's virtual doors by clicking my mouse.

I took a virtual tour of the Hermitage that took me through rooms from the ground floor to the very rooftops. A floor plan is available for each room. I clicked one room and a video image of the space transported me to another world. I almost felt as if I were walking through the room. When I spotted a piece of art that I wanted to view, I clicked on it.

I also made my way to the rooftops and gazed at stunning video views of the city of St. Petersburg.

Before leaving the Hermitage site, I visited the School Center. Children from ages 5 to 11 can **participate** in drawing classes at the museum. During my visit, I looked at the art that young artists **contributed** to an exhibition entitled "Our St. Petersburg." Each artwork in the exhibit illustrated a part of the **history** of this Russian seaport city.

Vocabulary

participate (pahr TIS uh PAYT) *v.* take part or share in an activity, event, or discussion

contribute (kuhn TRIB yoot) *v.* give or share money, knowledge, or ideas

history (HIS tuh ree) *n.* what has happened in the life or development of a people, country, or institution

The front of the Winter Palace, now the State Hermitage Museum, in St. Petersburg, Russia

This view shows the courtyard of the Isabella Stewart Gardner Museum with its beautiful flowers.

The Isabella Stewart Gardner Museum

Crisscrossing the globe in a nanosecond, I arrived in Boston. I paid a virtual visit to The Isabella Stewart Gardner Museum of Boston, Massachusetts.

The brick-and-mortar Gardner Museum is a small Venetian palace. Mrs. Gardner had this palace moved—brick by brick—from Italy. This unusual building sits across the street from a Boston park known as the Fens. Along the Fen's small river grow tall grasses, **cattails**, and other reeds. Inside the museum, a lovely courtyard garden blooms all year round.

Mrs. Gardner settled in Boston when she was about twenty. She loved art and traveled the world to collect it. She carefully arranged the works she collected in the rooms of her palace home. Before she died, Mrs. Gardner turned her home and its art collection into a museum. It was her wish that nothing in her museum be moved from the spot she had chosen for it. She also stated that nothing be added to the rooms. For decades the museum directors have honored her wishes. It hasn't always been easy.

One March night in 1990, thieves broke into the museum. They stole twelve pieces of art, including paintings by some of the world's most famous and revered artists. The **culprits** have still not been identified. The art has not yet been recovered. In the museum, empty frames where masterpieces once hung stare out. The frames have remained empty because of Mrs. Gardner's wish that nothing be added to her collection.

An 1888 oil painting of Isabella Stewart Gardner

Vocabulary

cattails (KAT taylz) *n.* tall reeds with furry, brown spikes, found in marshes and swamps

culprit (KUL prit) *n.* guilty person

However, in the virtual museum, you might say that some new work has been added to the museum. By running my mouse over the empty frames in the on-line rooms, I could make images of art appear in them. All of the artwork is by the contemporary artist Elaine Reichek. Her work never actually hung in the Gardner Museum. Creating online-only exhibits like the one I saw is one way that the Gardner continues to **thrive** in spite of its great loss.

Another view of the Gardner Museum courtyard

The Cybermuseum

Cybermuseums are art museums that open their virtual doors only in cyberspace. They have no brick-and-mortar buildings to house their collections. They exist only online.

The Greenmuseum site is one such museum. It collects environmental art. Most of this art is built and viewed outside. Environmental artists use the materials that they find in nature, such as snow or leaves. So, the art is often temporary because the materials don't last. However, the Greenmuseum site photographs these artworks in their natural surroundings and then exhibits the images online.

Mary Ellen Long is an environmental artist. Her work is part of the museum's collection. Long creates some of her artwork in the woods. When I visited the Greenmuseum site, I enjoyed viewing her sculpture called "Forest Room." I found that Long's art **evoked** in me feelings of peace and closeness to nature even though I was sitting in front of my computer in a noisy city.

Like the Greenmuseum site, the American Museum of Photography is a cybermuseum. Its website lists its location and hours of operation. The museum has a web address only but can be visited any day of the year, 24/7.

VOCABULARY

thrive (THRYV) *v.* do well; grow; prosper

evoke (ee VOHK) *v.* draw a feeling, idea, or reaction out of someone

53

When I visited, I made a virtual entrance into the Hall of Special Effects. There I viewed an exhibit called "Photographic Fictions: How the Camera Learned to Lie." I discovered that long before computer programs allowed people to alter images, photographers could "lie" with their cameras. More than one hundred years ago photographers used tricks to add images of imaginary figures to their photos. I'd like to find out how the 19th-century viewers **reacted** to that. When I looked at the photographs, I could hardly believe that anyone was fooled. But perhaps no one ever bothered to **check** for accuracy.

This photograph from the 1920s shows "people cowering in fear at the sight of a ghost."

This girl is viewing art from the Museum of Computer Art.

Another cybermuseum I explored is the Museum of Computer Art. As its name states, it is dedicated to art created on computers. During my visit there, I admired the work of an artist known as Skydancer. Like many of the artists on this site, Skydancer relies on the latest software and computer hardware to create elaborate images.

This online museum, like some others, encourages viewers to support its work by paying a membership fee. Members have access to special exhibits that casual visitors cannot see. Members can also submit their work to be considered for exhibition in the Guest Gallery. If you create computer art, you might want to join this museum and submit your latest masterpiece!

Vocabulary

react (ree AKT) *v.* behave in a particular way in response to someone or something

check (CHEK) *v.* confirm that something is true or accurate

By viewing art online, you can avoid the large crowds that sometimes pack art museums.

What Will the Future Bring?

Is a virtual visit to an art museum as good as—or maybe better than—being there? Will brick-and-mortar museums close their doors and exhibit only online? What would we miss if we couldn't walk among the great works of art?

For me, as amazing as a virtual visit can be, it will never replace the experience of standing before the original work of art. The real object that was touched by the artist's hand still evokes a feeling of awe. Although I have viewed Da Vinci's "Mona Lisa" on the Louvre's website, I still want to go to Paris, France, and stand face to face with the painting. Maybe she'll turn her famous and mysterious smile directly on me.

Discussion Questions

1. What purposes do art museums serve?

2. Think about a visit you have made to a brick-and-mortar art museum. Describe the experience, including how the kind of building and the way the art was displayed affected your reactions.

3. What do you like about visiting a virtual art museum? Describe the features on a museum website that help you to enjoy the art. Also discuss what you don't like about visiting an online museum.

4. Do you think that some day online museums might replace the brick-and-mortar museums? Explain why. Also describe any advantages and disadvantages of eliminating brick-and-mortar museums.

Testing the Market

Suppose you're starting a business. You've created a new product called Porto-Cup. Porto-Cup is the amazing, swiveling, self-sticking portable cup holder. You can stick Porto-Cup on your car, your desk, a wall—anywhere! You and your friends think Porto-Cup is terrific. In fact, everyone you've shown Porto-Cup to thinks it's terrific. So you're ready to go, right? Not quite.

When you asked your partners for money to place a factory order for Porto-Cups, they started to get nervous. It's not that they don't like Porto-Cup. It's just that ordering thousands of Porto-Cups will cost millions of dollars. Before they **contribute** money, your partners **inquire**, "How can you be sure that anyone will actually buy Porto-Cup?"

If you're being realistic, your answer is that you can't be sure. Selling a new product is always a **perilous** business. No one can ever **assume** success, and even the "best" product is never a sure bet. So what do you do now? You test the market. You do some market research.

Vocabulary

contribute (kuhn TRIB yoot) *v.* give or share money, knowledge, or ideas

inquire (in KWYR) *v.* ask

perilous (PER uh luhs) *adj.* dangerous

assume (uh SOOM) *v.* suppose something to be a fact; take on, as in a responsibility or role

59

What Is Market Research?

Market research is the process of gathering and analyzing information about a new or existing product. Businesses do market research for a variety of reasons. For example, companies test ideas for new products. Will they sell? They do market research to find out why an existing product is not selling. Through market research, companies discover what is **relevant** and **irrelevant** when it comes to selling a product. Market research answers the *who, what,* and *where* questions: Who are my customers? What do they want? What will they pay? Where do I find them?

People use market research because it allows them to test ideas and products before they **invest** a lot of money. Just about every kind of company and business you can think of uses market research. Car companies use it. Candidates for president use it. Hollywood moviemakers use it. So do makers of cell phones, lawn mowers, video games, breakfast cereals, and thousands of other things you buy and see every day.

This businesswoman reads a market research report on some of her company's products.

Last year, companies spent billions of dollars on market research. For them, the money was well spent because market research takes some doubt out of making business decisions. The research gives companies data about the products they sell. Business managers can make decisions based on solid facts. They don't have to **rely** on guesswork.

VOCABULARY

relevant (REL uh vuhnt) *adj.* having a logical connection with; relating to the point

irrelevant (ir REL uh vuhnt) *adj.* not having a connection with

invest (in VEST) *v.* put time, effort, or money into something to make it successful

rely (ree LY) *v.* trust or depend on someone or something

Market Analysis

Market research falls into two basic categories: competitor analysis and customer analysis. Competitor analysis asks questions about products on the market that are similar to your own product. Customer analysis asks questions about who customers are and what they want.

Competitor analysis is often the first kind of market research that a company does. Before you **launch** a product, it's usually a good idea to ask: "Does a product like this already exist? If so, how does it compare to my product?" For example, you might think Porto-Cup is a unique and completely new item. However, when you **analyze** the market, you might find other products that are very similar to Porto-Cup.

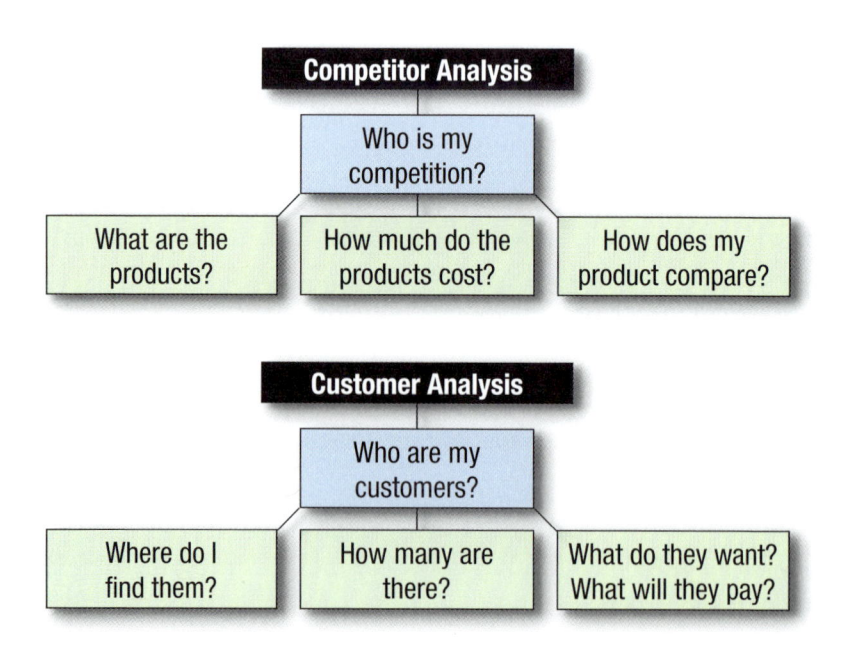

Competitor Analysis
- Who is my competition?
  - What are the products?
  - How much do the products cost?
  - How does my product compare?

Customer Analysis
- Who are my customers?
  - Where do I find them?
  - How many are there?
  - What do they want? What will they pay?

If similar products are out there, what should you do? Well, it all depends on the **data** you've collected. You may **discover** that the market is too crowded. Why waste energy trying to **impress** customers who already have a strong connection to an existing product? So you scrap your Porto-Cup plans and use your keen business **aptitude** to think up a new product idea.

On the other hand, competitor analysis might reveal that Porto-Cup has no real competition. This finding would appear to be good news. However, the situation now **requires** that you ask a new question: "Why aren't any competing products on the market?" Perhaps something is wrong with your original idea. Perhaps the competition knows something you don't know. What do you do now? Customer analysis.

Vocabulary

launch (LAWNCH) *v.* start something new; send off a ship, shuttle, or weapon

analyze (AN uh lyz) *v.* break something down into parts to examine it or determine its nature

data (DAY tuh) *n.* information or facts that have been gathered in order to be studied

discover (di SKUV er) *v.* find out

impress (im PRES) *v.* make someone feel admiration and respect; make clear the importance of something

aptitude (AP tuh tood) *n.* ability; talent

require (ree KWYR) *v.* demand by law; deem necessary

Customer Analysis

Customer analysis reveals who your customers are and what they want. Note that different products can have very different target audiences. You would not try to sell dog food to cat owners, for example. In a similar way, you need to find the customer base for the product you want to sell. Who are the customers who will buy Porto-Cups? Where do they live? How can you reach them—on TV? in newspaper ads? through the Internet?

Once you **identify** your customers, you probably want to learn how they feel about your product. However, getting them to **cooperate** in a market research study may not be as easy as it sounds. Most consumers lead busy lives with lots of **diversions**. So, you may have to offer them some kind of reward for giving you their time and opinions.

You can do this in a number of ways. You could offer free food and drinks as a way to get people to try Porto-Cup. Or, you could pay them to participate in a focus group.

Vocabulary

identify (eye DEN tuh FY) *v.* recognize something and be able to say what it is

cooperate (koh AHP er AYT) *v.* work together with others for a common purpose

diversions (duh VER zhuhnz) *n.* amusements; distractions

Companies need to identify which shoppers are likely to buy their products.

A focus group can let a company know how people feel about a new product.

The Focus Group

Focus groups are groups of people pulled together to explore their attitudes and opinions about a product or idea. Typically, a focus group consists of about 8 to 12 consumers.

Market researchers always need to make sure that the focus group is well balanced. What you want in a focus group is a good cross-section of your possible customer base. For example, you wouldn't want a focus group for cat food to be composed of ten dog owners. Neither would you want to test Porto-Cup on a group made up only of bike racers.

For Porto-Cup, testing a few bike racers would be fine. But racers might have trouble attaching Porto-Cup to the handlebars of their bikes. As a result, they might decide that Porto-Cup is not for them. To get a fair sampling of people for Porto-Cup, you would make sure to include a wide variety of possible customers.

The focus group, once together, typically meets for an hour or two. A moderator leads the discussion. This person does not state any opinions. Instead, the moderator learns the group's attitudes by asking **crucial** questions. "What do you like about the product?" "What don't you like?" "Which feature of the product caught your eye?"

As the discussion takes place, the client who wants the information often watches from behind a one-way mirror. The client can see the members of the focus group. The group cannot see the client.

The focus group can provide important information about a product. For example, look at the table that shows data resulting from Porto-Cup focus groups. Review the data. How might you change the product, based on the opinions of this focus group? One change you might consider would be to lower the price of Porto-Cup. Then, consumers might be more willing to buy a product they otherwise seem to like.

Vocabulary

crucial (KROO shuhl) *adj.* important; critical

Twelve-Member Focus Group Data for Porto-Cup			
	Group 1	Group 2	Group 3
Liked Porto-Cup idea	9	8	11
Porto-Cup is sturdy & well-made	10	9	9
Price is too high	11	10	12
Would use Porto-Cup	10	12	11
Would buy Porto-Cup	3	4	5

Market Testing

Another effective way to **evaluate** people's response to a product is to conduct a market test. In a market test, consumers test products for themselves. For example, suppose a company called Racerunner Broadband wants to test its Internet service. Racerunner can **obtain** data in three different ways.

First, the company can set up computers and let people try Racerunner. Second, they can set up a comparison test. In this method, test users compare Racerunner to its main competitor, called Starbright. Each product is identified so users can compare systems directly.

Finally, Racerunner can conduct a "blind" test. In this research, the products are not identified. Consumers don't know which system is which. Blind tests get rid of bias that users may have for or against a product.

Take a look at the results of the Racerunner tests. What conclusions can you draw about Racerunner? One might be that some customers were biased in favor of Starbright, the familiar name. Note that when the products were

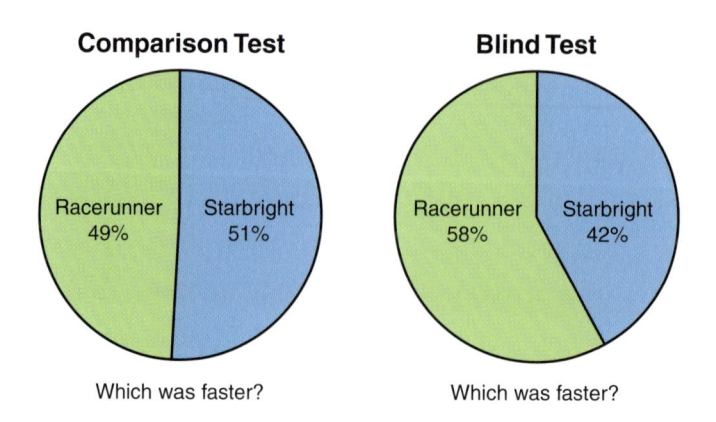

Comparison Test

Racerunner 49%
Starbright 51%

Which was faster?

Blind Test

Racerunner 58%
Starbright 42%

Which was faster?

labeled, Starbright was the winner. When the systems were not labeled, people thought that Racerunner was better. This finding suggests that people were judging the products by name, not by actual performance.

Keep this idea in mind when testing Porto-Cup or any new product. It's sometimes not enough just to have what you think is a better product. People tend to stick with what they know. So they tend to like brand name products. That's why it's so hard to introduce a new product like Porto-Cup. You're not just trying to catch people's attention. You're also trying to change their minds.

Many companies combine a market test with a focus group. The market test serves as a **preliminary** measure of consumer opinion. It contributes data about a product. Then the focus group asks people to **justify** their opinions and explain why they are **valid**.

Note that the Racerunner tests were only a part of a complete market research program. The company simply asked customers to decide which service was faster. In other tests, consumers might be asked to rate product features on a scale of 1 to 10. For example, they might score a broadband service for speed, ease of use, price, reliability, and so on.

VOCABULARY

evaluate (ee VAL yoo AYT) *v.* examine something to make a judgment

obtain (uhb TAYN) *v.* gain possession of something

preliminary (pree LIM uh NER ee) *adj.* coming before or leading up to the main action

justifies (JUS tuh fyz) *v.* excuses

valid (VAL id) *adj.* justifiable; logically correct

Once the testing is completed, market researchers must interpret the results they get. Sometimes, this task can be tricky. Take a look at how two well-known companies conducted market research and used the results.

Grey Poupon® versus French's®

In the mid-1980s, French's yellow mustard was found on almost every table in America. Then the Heublin Company decided to test its unknown mustard called Grey Poupon. Grey Poupon was everything French's was not. French's was plain. Grey Poupon was sophisticated. French's was bright yellow and made with vinegar. Grey Poupon had a muted brownish color and was made with imported white wine.

The Power and Pitfalls of Market Research

Before Grey Poupon TV Ads	French's Average Weekly Sales $210*
	Grey Poupon Weekly Sales $80*
After Grey Poupon TV Ads	French's Average Weekly Sales $172*
	Grey Poupon Weekly Sales $118*

* Amount of weekly sales in dollars at an average supermarket.

Market experts **predicted** that Americans would never buy a mustard like Grey Poupon. However, taste tests revealed an unexpected result. Americans loved Grey Poupon.

After Grey Poupon **achieved** high test scores, the company launched a series of famous commercials that featured two fancy Rolls Royces meeting on the road. In the commercial, one wealthy passenger leans out the window and says, "Pardon me. Would you have any Grey Poupon?"

The viewer sees the man in the second car holding a jar of Grey Poupon, next to a plate of beef.

The message was clear. Grey Poupon was an exceptional product that no one could do without.

After the company introduced the ads into new regions, sales of Grey Poupon skyrocketed. **Check** the data in the graph. By what percent did Grey Poupon sales increase after the ads were broadcast? If you came up with 47.5%, you did the math correctly. Who knows whether Grey Poupon would have ever become such a hot product if Heublin had not market tested it against French's.

Vocabulary

predict (pree DIKT) *v.* say in advance what you think will happen; foretell

achieve (uh CHEEV) *v.* succeed in doing something; accomplish; gain

check (CHEK) *v.* confirm that something is true or accurate

The Pepsi Challenge

In the 1980s, Coca-Cola was America's best-selling cola. Then Pepsi ran some blind taste tests against Coke. The tests took place in supermarkets. Shoppers stood at a counter and were given little plastic cups labeled "M" and "Q." Almost 6 out of 10 consumers preferred the cups labeled "M." "M" turned out to be Pepsi.

At first, Coke didn't believe the results of the Pepsi Challenge. Then the company ran its own tests. Coke found that people really did prefer Pepsi in blind tests! Coke responded by creating New Coke. New Coke was sweeter than old Coke and performed much better in taste tests.

Now another unexpected result showed up. Coke drinkers hated New Coke. Sales plummeted as customers demanded the return of old Coke. Within months, the company was forced to introduce Coca-Cola Classic, the old formula under a new name.

Pepsi Challenge Data (not the actual data)		
Number of testers who preferred—	M (Pepsi)	Q (Coke)
Test 1	89	76
Test 2	45	28
Test 3	109	72
Test 4	261	202
Total number of testers	502	378

*Data is exemplary and does not reflect actual data gathered in the study. The percentage difference in preferences, however, reflects the results shown in the study.

So how should we interpret the results of the Pepsi Challenge? Was the market research wrong? Look over the data in the table. What percent of the total preferred "M"? Yes, a whopping 57 percent preferred Pepsi.

After the New Coke disaster, Coke's marketers suspected that something was wrong with the Pepsi Challenge data. In fact, the studies had been solid. Coke's own tests also showed that people preferred Pepsi over Coke.

In the end, the Pepsi Challenge **demonstrated** the limits of market research. Or put it this way: conditions matter. In a supermarket taste test, people may have preferred Pepsi over Coke. Those conditions, however, were artificial. In real life, people do not stand at counters taking tiny sips of soft drinks from tiny plastic cups. They pour it into a tall glass, with ice, and sit back and relax.

When customers sampled colas under less artificial conditions, the results did change. In some tests, people were given a whole case of "Q" to drink at home. In those tests, Coke performed much better.

VOCABULARY

demonstrate (DEM uhn strayt) *v.* show or make clear by using examples or modeling

Lessons Learned

The Grey Poupon and Pepsi Challenge stories each provide a lesson for any growing business. Grey Poupon shows the power of market research. If knowledge is power, then market research is the ultimate kind of business knowledge. It tells you what will sell and what will not sell. The Pepsi Challenge seems to send the opposite message. Knowledge may be powerful, but it is no substitute for good old-fashioned common sense.

So, what should you do about the Porto-Cup? The table shows test data for the Porto-Cup against the leading portable cup, Umpty-Cup.

Based on the Porto-Cup challenge, should you go ahead and market your product? People seem to think Porto-Cup is easier to use and install than Umpty-Cup. Also, Porto-Cup can do one thing that Umpty-Cup can't do—swivel!

The Porto-Cup Challenge: Blind Tests		
Average score 1 = worst, 10 = best	Porto-Cup	Umpty-Cup
Quality	8.2	7.3
Ease to install, use	9.7	6.0
Spill control	7.9	8.5
Easy swivel	9.8	Not applicable
Overall	8.5	7.2

Shoppers have a large variety of products to choose from. Sometimes it's hard for companies to determine if a new product will be successful.

As you decide, keep in mind that in the Porto-Cup Challenge, as with the Pepsi Challenge, unseen forces might be at work. For example, Umpty-Cup might just have the perfect shape and feel that make customers love to drink out of it. Remember, too, that in the end your data is just a set of numbers. It's how you use those numbers that makes the difference.

Discussion Questions

1. What kinds of businesses conduct market research? What do they hope to find out from their research?

2. A company can spend millions of dollars on market research and still save money. How is this possible?

3. What is a focus group? Why can focus groups be a successful form of market research?

4. Why did New Coke fail? What could market researchers have done differently?

Glossary

achieve (uh CHEEV) *v.* succeed in doing something; accomplish; gain **37, 71**

analyze (AN uh lyz) *v.* break something down into parts to examine it or determine its nature **38, 44, 62**

anonymous (uh NAHN uh muhs) *adj.* by someone whose name is withheld or unknown; unacknowledged **7, 46**

aptitude (AP tuh tood) *n.* ability; talent **7, 63**

assume (uh SOOM) *v.* suppose something to be a fact; take on, as in a responsibility or role **28, 59**

cattails (KAT taylz) *n.* tall reeds with furry, brown spikes, found in marshes and swamps **50**

check (CHEK) *v.* confirm that something is true or accurate **30, 54, 71**

communal (kuh MYOON uhl) *adj.* shared by all **16**

connect (kuh NEKT) *v.* to join or be joined **12**

conserve (kuhn SERV) *v.* keep from being damaged, lost, or wasted; save **46**

contribute (kuhn TRIB yoot) *v.* give or share money, knowledge, or ideas **32, 49, 59**

cooperate (koh AHP er AYT) *v.* work together with others for a common purpose **9, 64**

crucial (KROO shuhl) *adj.* important; critical **4, 28, 67**

culprit (KUL prit) *n.* guilty person **51**

data (DAY tuh) *n.* information or facts that have been gathered in order to be studied **63**

define (dee FYN) *v.* set clear boundaries or distinct characteristics **39**

demonstrate (DEM uhn strayt) *v.* show or make clear by using examples or modeling **31, 73**

desolate (DES uh lit) *adj.* lonely; solitary **9**

discover (di SKUV er) *v.* find out **63**

discovery (di SKUV uh ree) *n.* a fact, thing, or answer to a question that someone discovers, or finds **9**

distinct (dis TINKT) *adj.* separate and different **26**

diversions (duh VER zhuhnz) *n.* amusements; distractions **64**

elaboration (ee LAB uh RAY shuhn) *n.* adding of more details **44**

emphasize (EM fuh syz) *v.* stress something in order to make it stand out **15, 30**

enable (en AY buhl) *v.* make able; authorize, allow, or permit **4, 26**

enrich (en RICH) *v.* give more value or effectiveness to **4, 42**

envision (en VIZH uhn) *v.* picture in one's mind **26, 41**

evaluate (ee VAL yoo AYT) *v.* examine something to make a judgment **19, 68**

evoke (ee VOHK) *v.* draw a feeling, idea, or reaction out of someone **53**

examine (eg ZAM uhn) *v.* look at carefully in order to find out the facts and condition of something; inspect **46**

expedition (eks puh DI shuhn) *n.* journey taken for a specific purpose **42**

explore (eks PLOHR) *v.* look into closely; examine carefully **4**

focus (FOH kuhs) *v.* to fix or concentrate on one thing; adjust to make clear **4, 44**

frontier (fruhn TEER) *n.* the developing, often uncivilized, region of a country; any new field of learning **24**

gauge (GAYJ) *v.* estimate; judge **24**

hindered (HIN derd) *v.* held back **8, 42**

history (HIS tuh ree) *n.* what has happened in the life or development of a people, country, or institution **49**

77

identify (eye DEN tuh FY) *v.* recognize something and be able to say what it is **10, 22, 44, 64**

impetus (IM puh tuhs) *n.* driving force **9**

impress (im PRES) *v.* make someone feel admiration and respect; make clear the importance of something **44, 63**

indispensable (IN di SPEN suh buhl) *adj.* absolutely necessary; can't be thrown away **29**

information (in fuhr MAY shuhn) *n.* knowledge; facts; data **42**

inquire (in KWYR) *v.* ask **59**

insignificant (IN sig NIF i kuhnt) *adj.* having little or no meaning **8**

invest (in VEST) *v.* put time, effort, or money into something to make it successful **60**

investigate (in VES tuh GAYT) *v.* examine an object or situation in order to gain information **10**

irrelevant (ir REL uh vuhnt) *adj.* not having a connection with **60**

justifies (JUS tuh fyz) *v.* excuses **69**

launch (LAWNCH) *v.* start something new; send off a ship, shuttle, or weapon **26, 42, 62**

museum (myoo ZEE uhm) *n.* institution, building, or room for preserving and exhibiting artistic, historical, or scientific objects **41**

navigate (NAV uh gayt) *v.* steer, or direct, a ship or aircraft **26**

obtain (uhb TAYN) *v.* gain possession of something **28, 68**

optimist (AHP tuh mist) *n.* someone who takes the most hopeful view of matters **32**

parallel (PAR uh lel) *adj.* extending in the same direction and at the same distance apart **30**

participate (pahr TIS uh PAYT) *v.* take part or share in an activity, event, or discussion **49**

perilous (PER uh luhs) *adj.* dangerous **59**

predict (pree DIKT) *v.* say in advance what you think will happen; foretell **32, 71**

preliminary (pree LIM uh NER ee) *adj.* coming before or leading up to the main action **69**

presume (pree ZOOM) *v.* accept something as true until proven otherwise **7**

profusely (proh FYOOS lee) *adv.* freely; plentifully; excessively **5**

promote (pruh MOHT) *v.* encourage; contribute to the growth of; raise to a higher level or rank **42**

radiant (RAY dee uhnt) *adj.* shining brightly **5**

react (ree AKT) *v.* behave in a particular way in response to someone or something **5, 54**

relevant (REL uh vuhnt) *adj.* having a logical connection with; relating to the point **15, 60**

rely (ree LY) *v.* trust or depend on someone or something **7, 28, 46, 61**

require (ree KWYR) *v.* demand by law; deem necessary **32, 63**

significant (sig NIF i kuhnt) *adj.* having an important meaning **5, 28, 42**

thrive (THRYV) *v.* do well; grow; prosper **52**

transport (tranz POHRT) *v.* to carry or move from one place to another **8, 41**

ultimate (UHL tuh mit) *adj.* final; last or highest possible **24**

79

understand (un duhr STAND) *v.* get or perceive the meaning of; know or grasp what is meant; comprehend **25**

undertake (UN her TAYK) *v.* take on or agree to do a difficult or lengthy task **32, 46**

unearthed (un ERTHD) *v.* dug up **10**

valid (VAL id) *adj.* justifiable; logically correct **69**

Photo Credits

Cover: © Herbert Spichtinger/zefa/CORBIS; **4–5:** © Eyebyte/Alamy; **6–7:** © Map Resources 2007; **6–7: m.** © John Martin/Alamy; **8–9:** © Stockpile/Alamy; **10–11:** © AP Photo/Aerial-Cam for National Geographic, Adam Stanford; **12–13:** © Richard T. Nowitz/CORBIS; **14:** Ground plan of Stonehenge, engraved by James Basire, from Sir Richard Colt Hoare's 'The History of Ancient Wiltshire', London, 1810-11 (engraving) by Philip Crocker (18th century) © Private Collection/© Dreweatt Neate Fine Art Auctioneers, Newbury, Berks, UK/The Bridgeman Art Library; **16–17:** © Liquid Light/Alamy; **17:** © Greenhalf Photography/CORBIS; **18–19:** © Paul Barton/CORBIS; **20–21:** © Robert Harding Picture Library Ltd/Alamy; **22:** © NASA/Corbis; **22–23:** © NASA/Corbis; **24:** © Image Source/SuperStock; **29:** © Réunion des Musées Nationaux/Art Resource, NY; **30–31:** ©Visual Arts Library (London)/Alamy; **32–33:** © John Harrison (1693-1776) 1767 (oil on canvas) by Thomas King (d.1769) © Science Museum, London, UK/The Bridgeman Art Library; **36–37:** © Digitalglobe via CNP/CNP/Corbis; **38–39:** © Hugh Threlfall/Alamy; **40:** Image © Andy Warhol Foundation/CORBIS and Artwork © The Andy Warhol Foundation for the Visual Arts/Corbis; **42–43:** © Steve Hamblin/Alamy; **45:** © The Metropolitan Museum of Art/Art Resource, NY; **46:** © Ross Pictures/CORBIS; **48–49:** © Richard T. Nowitz/Corbis; **50–51:** © Rough Guides/Alamy; **51:** © Isabella Stewart Gardner (1840-1924), 1888 (oil on canvas) by John Singer Sargent (1856-1925) © Isabella Stewart Gardner Museum, Boston, MA, USA/The Bridgeman Art Library; **52:** ©Tony Arruza/CORBIS; **54–55:** © NMPFT/Kodak Collection/SSPL/The Image Works; **55:** © LWA-Dann Tardif/CORBIS; **56–57:** © Dattatreya/Alamy; **58–59:** © Don Bishop/Photodisc/Getty Images; **58–59: m.** © Stockbyte/Getty Images; **60–61:** © age fotostock/SuperStock; **61:** © Image Source/Corbis; **64–65:** © SUNNYphotography.com/Alamy; **66–67:** © Randy Faris/Corbis; **70:** © Envision/Corbis; **73:** © foodfolio/Alamy; **74–75:** © Corbis Premium Collection/Alamy